To

_____

From

_____

Little Book

DEVOTIONS
31 DAILY DEVOTIONALS

Forgiveness

Little Book

DEVOTIONS

Forgiveness

The quoted ideas expressed in this book (but not scripture verses) are not, in all cases, exact quotations, as some have been edited for clarity and brevity. In all cases, the author has attempted to maintain the speaker's original intent. In some cases, quoted material for this book was obtained from secondary sources, primarily print media. While every effort was made to ensure the accuracy of these sources, the accuracy cannot be guaranteed. For additions, deletions, corrections or clarifications in future editions of this text, please write BRIGHTON BOOKS.

The Holy Bible, King James Version

The Holy Bible, New King James Version (NKJV) Copyright © 1982 by Thomas Nelson, Inc. Used by permission.

New Century Version®. (NCV) Copyright © 1987, 1988, 1991 by Word Publishing, a division of Thomas Nelson, Inc. All rights reserved. Used by permission.

International Children's Bible®, New Century Version®. (ICB) Copyright © 1986, 1988, 1999 by Tommy Nelson™, a division of Thomas Nelson, Inc. All rights reserved. Used by permission.

The Holman Christian Standard Bible™ (HCSB) Copyright © 1999, 2000, 2001 by Holman Bible Publishers. Used by permission.

The prayers and essays in this book are written by Criswell Freeman; used with permission.

Compiled and Edited: Mary Susan Freeman
Cover Design: Kim Russel, Wahoo Designs
Page Layout: Bart Dawson

ISBN 1-58334-224-9
Printed in the United States of America

For All of God's Children

Table of Contents

A Message to Parents

Congratulations on picking up this book! It proves that you're a thoughtful parent who is interested in both the spiritual and intellectual development of your child.

This little book can be an important addition to your family's library if you take the time to read it with your child. This text is intended to be read by Christian parents to their young children. The book contains 31 brief chapters, one for each day of the month. Each chapter is composed of a Bible verse, a brief story, helpful hints for kids and for parents, and a prayer. Every chapter examines some aspect of an important Biblical theme: forgiveness.

For the next 31 days, try this experiment: read one chapter each night to your child, and then spend a few more moments talking about the chapter's meaning. By the end of the month, you will have had 31 different opportunities to share God's wisdom with your son or daughter, and that's a very good thing.

If you have been touched by God's love and His grace, then you know the joy that He has brought into your own life. Now it's your turn to share His message with the boy or girl whom He has entrusted to your care. Happy reading! And may God richly bless you and your family, now and forever.

Forgiveness

.

God Asks Us to Forgive

Yes, if you forgive others for the things
they do wrong, then your Father
in heaven will also forgive you
for the things you do wrong.

❀ ❀ ❀

Matthew 6:14 ICB

The Bible tells us this: When other people do things that are wrong, we should forgive them. God's Word also tells us that when we're willing to forgive others, God is quick to forgive us for the mistakes that we make.

Has somebody done something that makes you angry? Talk things over with your mom or dad, and then be ready to forgive the person who has hurt your feelings. And remember: God wants you to hurry up and forgive others, just like God is always in a hurry to forgive you.

Making up may not be as hard as you think! If there is someone who has been unkind to you, perhaps it's time for the two of you to make up. If you're willing to be the first person to say something nice, you'll discover that making up is usually easier than you think.

WOW

When God forgives, He forgets. He buries our sins in the sea and puts a sign on the shore saying, "No Fishing Allowed." Let's forgive other people in the very same way.

Corrie ten Boom

Becoming a model of forgiveness: If you want your children to learn the art of forgiveness, then you must master that art yourself. If you're able to forgive those who have hurt you and, by doing so, move on with your life, your kids will learn firsthand that forgiveness is God's way.

19

Dear Lord,
You have forgiven me.
Now, it's my turn to forgive
others. Help me fill my heart
with kind thoughts, and help me
fill each day with good deeds.
Thank you, Lord, for Your love,
for Your forgiveness,
and for Your Son Jesus.

Amen

What It Means
to Forgive

Peter said to them,
"Change your hearts and lives . . .
in the name of Jesus Christ."

❀ ❀ ❀

Acts 2:38 NCV

What does it mean to forgive? Forgiveness means that you decide to change your angry thoughts into kind thoughts. Forgiveness means that you decide not to stay mad at somebody who has done something wrong. Forgiveness happens when you decide that obeying God is more important than staying angry.

Sometimes forgiveness can be very hard, but it's the right thing to do. Why? Because forgiveness is God's way, and you should make it your way, too!

When in doubt . . . talk it out! If you're uncertain about a particular situation, talk it over with your parents. They'll help you decide how to handle things in the best way. So if you have a doubt about it, talk about it . . . **Now**!

WOW
If God forgives you and me,
how can you withhold your forgiveness
from someone else?
Anne Graham Lotz

Holding a grudge? Drop it! How can you expect your kids to forgive others if you don't? Never expect your children to be more forgiving than you are.

23

PRAY TIME

Dear Lord,
today I am going to forgive
others. When I forgive other
people, I know that I am
obeying your instructions.
And I know that I am also
getting rid of angry feelings
that can hurt me more than they
hurt anybody else. So today,
I will forgive and keep forgiving,
just like You always forgive me.

Amen

When Forgiveness Is Hard

I tell you, love your enemies.
Pray for those who hurt you.
If you do this, you will be true sons
of your Father in heaven.

✻ ✻ ✻

Matthew 6:44-45 ICB

Is forgiving someone else an easy thing for you to do or a hard thing? If you're like most people, forgiving others can be hard, Hard, HARD! But even if you're having a very hard time forgiving someone, you can do it if you talk things over with your parents, and if you talk things over with God.

Do you find forgiveness difficult? Talk about it and pray about it. You'll feel better when you do.

If you're having trouble forgiving someone else . . . think how many times other people have forgiven you!

WOW

When God tells us to love our enemies,
He gives, along with the command,
the love that we need to forgive them.

Corrie ten Boom

If it were easy: If forgiveness were easy, everybody would be doing it. Of course, forgiveness can, at times, be a very hard thing to do. So be quick to explain to your child that forgiving another person—even when it's difficult—is the correct thing to do.

Dear Lord,
I can be so impatient,
and I can become so angry.
Calm me down, Lord, and help me
become a more patient, forgiving
Christian. Just as You have
forgiven me, Father, let me
forgive others so that I can
follow the example of Your Son.

Amen

Do unto 4 Others

Do for other people the same things
you want them to do for you.

❋ ❋ ❋

Matthew 7:12 ICB

The words of Matthew 7:12 remind us that, as believers in Christ, we should treat others as we wish to be treated. This is called the Golden Rule, but for Christians, it's worth much more than gold.

Do you want other people to forgive you when you make mistakes? Of course you do. And that's why you should be willing to forgive them.

The Golden Rule should be your tool for deciding how you will treat others. So use the Golden Rule as your guide for living and forgiving!

The next time you're standing in line, don't try to push ahead of your neighbors. After all, if you don't want other people breaking in line in front of you, then you shouldn't break in line in front of them!

WOW
Forgiveness is contagious.
First you forgive them, and pretty soon, they'll forgive you, too.
Marie T. Freeman

Parent Tip

You are an example; be a good one: Your children will learn how to treat others by watching you; be kindhearted, understanding, and forgiving to everyone, starting with the precious people who live under your roof.

Dear Lord,
help me always to do my
very best to treat others as
I wish to be treated.
The Golden Rule is Your rule,
Father; let me also make it mine.

Amen

How Often Should We Forgive?

5

Then Peter came to Jesus and asked, "Lord, when my fellow believer sins against me, how many times must I forgive him? Should I forgive him as many as seven times?" Jesus answered, "I tell you, you must forgive him more than seven times. You must forgive him even if he does wrong to you seventy-seven times."

❊ ❊ ❊

Matthew 18:21-22 NCV

If you forgive somebody once, that's enough, right? WRONG!!! Even if you've forgiven somebody many times before, you must keep on forgiving. Jesus teaches us that we must keep forgiving people even if they continue to misbehave. Why? Because we, too, need to be forgiven over and over again. And if God keeps forgiving us, then we must be willing to do the same thing for others.

Forgive . . . and keep forgiving! Sometimes, you may forgive someone once, and then, at a later time, become angry at the very same person again. If so, you must forgive that person again and again . . . until it sticks!

WOW

How often should you forgive the other person? Only as many times as you want God to forgive you!

Marie T. Freeman

It starts at home . . . and as the parent, you're in charge of demonstrating the fine art of forgiveness. It's a big job, so don't be afraid to ask for help . . . especially God's help.

Dear Lord,
thank You for loving me
and forgiving me. I will return
Your love by sharing it . . .
today and every day.

Amen

Forgive and Forget?

He has taken our sins away from us
as far as the east is from west.

❋ ❋ ❋

Psalm 103:12 ɪᴄʙ

Have you heard the saying, "Forgive and forget"? Well, it's certainly easier said than done. It's easy to talk about forgiving somebody, but actually forgiving that person can be much harder to do. And when it comes to forgetting, forget about it!

Sometimes, it's impossible to forget the people who hurt our feelings. But even if we can't forget, we can forgive. And that's exactly what God teaches us to do.

What's good for you is good for them, too: If you want others to try their best to "forgive and forget" your mistakes, then you should do the same for them.

WOW
God forgets the past. Imitate him.
Max Lucado

Parent Tip

Help from the sidelines: As parents, we can't make our children forgive others, but we can coach them on the art of forgiveness. All of us, whether youngsters or grown-ups, learn the art of forgiveness when we learn to treat others as we wish to be treated. And if that sounds suspiciously like the Golden Rule, that's because it is the Golden Rule.

Dear Lord,
it's so easy to judge other
people, but it's also easy to
misjudge them. Only You can
judge a human heart, Lord,
so let me love my friends and
let me forgive them when they
make mistakes, but never
let me make the mistake
of judging them; instead,
I'll leave judging up to You.

Amen

7
Forgiving Family

Whoever brings trouble with his family
will be left with nothing but the wind.

❀ ❀ ❀

Proverbs 11:29 ICB

Sometimes, it's easy to become angry with the people we love most, and sometimes it's hard to forgive them. After all, we know that our family will still love us no matter how angry we become. But while it's easy to become angry at home, it's usually wrong.

The next time you're tempted to stay angry at a brother or a sister or a parent, remember that these are the people who love you more than anybody else! Then, calm down, and forgive them . . . NOW! Because peace is always beautiful, especially when it's peace at your house.

Since you love your family . . . let them know it by the things you say and the things you do. And, never take your family members for granted; they deserve your very best treatment!

WOW
There is always room for more loving forgiveness within our homes.

James Dobson

Parent Tip

You may become angry, but . . . Of course, you will experience times when you feel anger toward family members, but your love for them should never be in question. Our love for our families must never be turned on and off like the garden hose; it should, instead, flow like a mighty river, too deep to touch bottom and too strong to stop.

Dear Lord,
You have given me a wonderful
gift: a loving family. Today and
every day, let me show my
family that I love them by
the words that I speak
and the way that I behave.

Amen

Imitating Jesus

8

This is what you were called to do,
because Christ suffered for you
and gave you an example to follow.
So you should do as he did.

❈ ❈ ❈

1 Peter 2:21 NCV

If you're not certain whether something is right or wrong, ask yourself a simple question: "How would Jesus behave if He were here?" The answer to that question will tell you what to do.

Jesus was perfect, but we are not. Still, we must try as hard as we can to be like Him. When we do, we will love others, just like Christ loves us.

Someone very near you may need a helping hand or a kind word, so keep your eyes open, and look for people who need your help, whether at home, at church, or at school.

WOW
We hurt people by being too busy,
too busy to notice their needs.
Billy Graham

Parent Tip

Preach, teach, and reach . . . out!: When it comes to teaching our children how to become faithful servants of Christ, our sermons are not as important as our service. Charity should start at home—with parents—and work its way down the family tree from there.

Dear Lord,
when I am uncertain what to do,
let me look to Jesus as my
example. Let me do my best
to behave like Jesus would
behave if He were in my place.
Thank You, Lord, for a perfect
example of the perfect way
to behave; that example
is Your Son.

Amen

Nobody's Perfect

For all have sinned and fall short
of the glory of God.

❖ ❖ ❖

Romans 3:23 HCSB

Do you make mistakes? Of course you do . . . everybody does. When you make a mistake, you must try your best to learn from it so that you won't make the very same mistake again. And, if you have hurt someone—or if you have disobeyed God—you must ask for forgiveness.

Remember: mistakes are a part of life, but the biggest mistake you can make is to keep making the same mistake over and over and over again.

Made a mistake? Ask for forgiveness? If you've broken one of God's rules, you can always ask Him for His forgiveness. And He will always give it!

WOW

There is no one so far lost that Jesus cannot find him and cannot save him.

Andrew Murray

Parents aren't perfect: The perfect parent does not exist. So don't be too hard on yourself when you fall short of absolute perfection. Do your best, and trust God with the rest.

Dear Lord,
thank You for loving me,
even when I make mistakes.
You forgive me, Lord, and so do
my parents. Let me learn
to forgive others, so that
I can treat other people in
the very same way that
I have been treated.

Amen

10

When We're Angry

A wise person is patient.
He will be honored if he ignores
a wrong done against him.

❋ ❋ ❋

Proverbs 19:11 ICB

When you're angry, you will be tempted to say things and do things that you'll regret later. But don't do them! Instead of doing things in a hurry, slow down long enough to calm yourself down.

Jesus does not intend that you strike out against other people, and He doesn't intend that your heart be troubled by anger. Your heart should instead be filled with love, just like Jesus' heart was . . . and is!

Time out!: If you become angry, the time to step away from the situation is before you say unkind words or do unkind things—not after. It's perfectly okay to place yourself in "time out" until you can calm down.

WOW

When you strike out in anger,
you may miss the other person,
but you will always hit yourself.

Jim Gallery

Don't fan the flames: When your children become angry or upset, you'll tend to become angry and upset, too. Resist that temptation. As the grown-up person in the family, it's up to you to remain calm, even when other, less mature, members of the family can't.

Dear Lord,
I can be so impatient, and
I can become so angry.
Calm me down, Lord, and help me
be a patient, forgiving Christian.
Just as You have forgiven me,
Father, let me forgive others
so that I can follow
the example of Your Son.

Amen

11

Understanding the Other Person

If it costs everything you have,
get understanding.

❈ ❈ ❈

Proverbs 4:7 NCV

There's an old saying that goes something like this: "Try to put yourself in the other person's shoes." It means that the more you understand somebody, the easier it is to forgive that person.

When you become angry with someone, try putting yourself in the other person's shoes. When you do, perhaps you'll be a little bit more understanding—and a little bit quicker to forgive.

Respecting all kinds of people: Make sure that you show proper respect for everyone, even if that person happens to be different from you. It's easy to make fun of people who seem different . . . but it's wrong.

WOW

The old saying is true: People don't care what we know until they know we care.

Rick Warren

Parent Tip

It starts with you: Remember: Kindness, dignity, and respect for others begins at the head of the household and works its way down from there. And our kids are always watching!

Dear Lord,
let me be an understanding
person, especially to my family
and friends. Let me be kind
to those who need my
encouragement and let me be
a helpful, generous Christian
today and every day.

Amen

12
Forgiving Friends

It is good and pleasant when God's people
live together in peace!

❋ ❋ ❋

Psalm 133:1 NCV

The Bible tells us that friendship can be a wonderful thing. That's why it's good to know how to make and to keep good friends. And one way that we keep friends is to forgive them when they make mistakes.

If you want to make lots of friends, practice the Golden Rule with everybody you know. Be kind. Share. Say nice things. Be quick to forgive, and be helpful. When you do, you'll discover that the Golden Rule isn't just a nice way to behave; it's also a great way to make and to keep friends!

Everybody is a VIP: VIP means "Very Important Person." To God, everybody is a VIP, and we should treat every person with dignity, patience, and respect.

WOW
We cannot be "right" with God until we are "right" with one another.
Charles Swindoll

It takes time and understanding! Sometimes our children are impatient to build their friendships. Make sure that your child understands that it takes time, effort, and understanding to build friendships that last.

Dear Lord,
when somebody hurts my
feelings, let me be patient
and kind. And when a friend
does something wrong, help me
do the right thing by offering
my forgiveness sooner
rather than later!

Amen

13
When We're Tired

The Lord gives strength to those
who are tired.

❋ ❋ ❋

Isaiah 40:29 ICB

Some rules are easier to understand than they are to live by. Jesus told us that we should treat other people in the same way that we would want to be treated: that's the Golden Rule. But sometimes, especially when we're tired or upset, that rule is very hard to follow.

Jesus wants us to treat other people with respect, kindness, and love. When we do, we make our families and friends happy . . . and we make our Father in heaven very proud. So if you're wondering how to treat someone else, ask the person you see every time you look into the mirror. The answer you receive will tell you exactly what to do.

Rest, rest, rest . . . Oftentimes, our anger is nothing more than exhaustion in disguise. When in doubt, get a good night's sleep.

WOW
You can't do your best if you're tired.
See that your clock does not run down.
Mrs. Charles E. Cowman

Parent tip

Grownups need sleep, too . . . Most adults need about eight hours of sleep each night. If you're depriving yourself of much needed sleep in order to stay up and watch late night television, you've developed a bad habit. Instead, do yourself a favor: turn off the TV and go to bed.

Dear Lord,
when I'm tired, give me
the wisdom to do the smart
thing: give me the wisdom to put
my head on my pillow and rest!

Amen

14

When People Aren't Nice

Whoever forgives someone's sin
makes a friend . . . .

❋ ❋ ❋

Proverbs 17:9 NCV

Face it: sometimes people aren't nice. And when other people are unkind to you, or they are unkind to someone you love, you may be tempted to strike out in anger. Don't do it! Instead, remember that God corrects other people's behaviors in His own way, and He probably doesn't need your help. And remember that God has commanded you to forgive other people, just as you seek forgiveness from others when you misbehave.

So, when other people aren't nice, forgive them as quickly as you can. And leave the rest up to God.

Stand up and be counted! Do you know children who say or do cruel things to other kids? If so, don't join in! Instead, stand up for those who need your help. It's the right thing to do.

WOW
Our pain is with us for a little while.
Our God is with us forever.
Marie T. Freeman

When kids are mean: Let's face it: even the most angelic children can do things that are unfair or unkind. When we observe such behavior in our own children, we must be understanding but firm. We live in a world where misbehavior is tolerated and, in many cases, glorified. But inside the walls of our own homes, misbehavior should not be ignored; it should be corrected by loving, courageous parents.

71

Dear Lord,
sometimes it's very hard
to forgive those who have
hurt me, but with Your help,
I can forgive them. Help me to
bring forgiveness into my heart,
so that I can forgive others just
as You have already forgiven me.

Amen

15
Learning to Be Patient

Always be humble and gentle. Be patient
and accept each other with love.

❋ ❋ ❋

Ephesians 4:2 ICB

Jesus teaches us the Golden Rule for living: We should treat other people in the same way that we want to be treated. And because we want other people to be patient with us, we, in turn, must be patient with them.

Being patient with other people means treating them with kindness, respect, and understanding. It means forgiving our friends when they've done something we don't like. Sometimes, it's hard to be patient, but we've got to do our best. And when we do, we're following the Golden Rule—God's rule for how to treat others—and everybody wins!

It's your turn . . . God and your parents have been patient with you . . . now it's your turn to be patient with others.

WOW

If only we could be as patient
with other people as God is with us!

Jim Gallery

Imitating Him while imitating you: Kids imitate their parents, so act accordingly! The best way for your children to learn how to follow in Christ's footsteps is by following you while you follow Him!

Dear Lord,
sometimes it's hard to be
patient, and that's exactly when
I should try my hardest to be
patient. Help me to obey You by
being a patient, loving person . . .
even when it's hard.

Amen

16

Asking for Forgiveness

But if we confess our sins, he will forgive
our sins, because we can trust God to do
what is right. He will cleanse us from
all the wrongs we have done.

❋ ❋ ❋

1 John 1:9 NCV

When you make a mistake or hurt someone's feelings, what should you do? You should say you're sorry and ask for forgiveness. And you should do so sooner, not later.

The longer you wait to apologize, the harder it is on you. So if you've done something wrong, don't be afraid to ask for forgiveness, and don't be afraid to ask for it NOW!

Sorry you said it? Apologize! Did you say something that hurt someone's feelings? Then it's time for an apology: yours. It's never too late to apologize, but it's never too early, either!

WOW

God sees everything we've ever done
and He's willing to forgive.
But we must confess to him.

Ruth Bell Graham

Parent Tip

When it's over, it's over . . . When your child sincerely apologizes and makes amends, then it's time for you, as the parent, to demonstrate the art of forgiveness—and the art of creative forgetfulness—by accepting your child's apology and moving on.

Dear Lord,
when I make mistakes,
I will admit what I've done,
and I will apologize to the people
I've hurt. You are perfect, Lord;
I am not. I thank You for Your
forgiveness and for Your love.

Amen

17

From the Heart

Create in me a pure heart, God,
and make my spirit right again.

❋ ❋ ❋

Psalm 51:10 NCV

Where does forgiveness start? It starts in our hearts and works its way out from there. Jesus taught us that a pure heart is a wonderful blessing. It's up to each of us to fill our hearts with love for God, love for Jesus, and love for all people. When we do, we are blessed.

Do you want to be the best person you can be? Then invite the love of Christ into your heart and share His love with your family and friends. And remember that lasting love always comes from a pure heart . . . like yours!

Show them how you feel: It's good to tell your loved ones how you feel about them, but that's not enough. You should also show them how you feel with your good deeds and your kind words.

WOW

You cannot be the person God meant you to be, and you cannot live the life He meant you to live, unless you live from the heart.

John Eldredge

Learning from a heart like yours . . . Your children will learn how to treat others by watching you (not by listening to you!). Your own genuine acts of kindness and forgiveness will speak far louder than your words.

Dear Lord,
You have given me the gift
of love; let me share that gift
with others. And, keep me
mindful that the essence
of love is not to receive it,
but to give it, today and forever.

Amen

18

Don't Be Cruel

A kind person is doing himself a favor.
But a cruel person brings
trouble upon himself.

❈ ❈ ❈

Proverbs 11:17 ICB

Sometimes, young people can be very mean. They may make fun of other people, and when they do so, it's wrong. Period.

As Christians, we should be kind to everyone. And, if other kids say unkind things to a child or make fun of him or her, it's up to us to step in and lend a helping hand.

Today and every day, be a person who is known for your kindness, not for your cruelty. That's how God wants you to behave. Period.

Don't be cruel: Sometimes, you can be too honest, especially if you say unkind things that are intended to hurt other people's feelings. When you're deciding what to say, you should mix honesty and courtesy together. When you do, you'll say the right thing.

WOW
Brotherly love is still the distinguishing badge of every true Christian.
Matthew Henry

Play fair: Never try to win an argument by hurting another person; it's simply not worth it. Besides, your kids are probably watching.

Dear Lord,
sometimes people are cruel.
Let me never be such a person.
Let me treat others as I wish to
be treated, and let my thoughts
and actions honor you
today and forever.

Amen

19

Playing by the Rules: God's Rules

But the truly happy person is the one who carefully studies God's perfect law that makes people free. He continues to study it. He listens to God's teaching and does not forget what he heard. Then he obeys what God's teaching says. When he does this, it makes him happy.

❀ ❀ ❀

James 1:25 ICB

We know that it's right to forgive other people and wrong to stay angry with them. But sometimes, it's so much easier to do the wrong thing than it is to do the right thing, especially when we're tired or frustrated. When you do the right thing by forgiving other people, you'll feel good because you'll know that you're obeying God. And that's a very good feeling indeed. So make this promise to yourself and keep it: play by the rules—God's rules. You'll always be glad you did.

Sometimes happy, sometimes not: Even if you're a very good person, you shouldn't expect to be happy all the time. Sometimes, things will happen to make you sad, and it's okay to be sad when bad things happen to you or to your friends or family. But remember: through good times and bad, you'll always be happier if you obey the rules of your Father in heaven. So obey them!

WOW

Obedience is the natural outcome
of belief.

C. H. Spurgeon

Logical consequences! The world won't protect your child from the consequences of misbehavior, and neither should you. As a parent, your job is to ensure that the consequences of your child's actions are logical, measured, appropriate, and thoroughly understood by your youngster.

Dear Lord,
Your laws are right for me;
let me live by those laws.
And, let me be a good example
for others so that they, too,
might follow in the footsteps
of Your Son Jesus.

Amen

Teaching Others by Example

You are young, but do not let anyone
treat you as if you were not important.
Be an example to show the believers how
they should live. Show them with
your words, with the way you live,
with your love, with your faith,
and with your pure life.

❋ ❋ ❋

1 Timothy 4:12 ICB

What kind of example are you? Are you the kind of person who shows other people what it means to be kind and forgiving? Hopefully so!!!

How hard is it to say a kind word? Not very! How hard is it to accept someone's apology? Usually not too hard. So today, be a good example for others to follow. Because God needs people, like you, who are willing to stand up and be counted for Him. And that's exactly the kind of example you should try to be.

Cheerfulness by example. Do you need a little cheering up? If so, find somebody else who needs cheering up, too. Then, do your best to brighten that person's day. When you do, you'll discover that cheering up other people is a wonderful way to cheer yourself up, too!

WOW
More depends on my walk than my talk.
D. L. Moody

Your life is a sermon: preach and teach accordingly: The sermons you live are far more important than the ones you preach. Make no mistake, your kids are watching carefully and learning constantly.

Dear Lord,
You have wonderful plans for me,
and You know the kind of person
You want me to become.
Let me be that kind of person.
And let me be the right kind
of example for my friends
and family—today and every day.

Amen

21

Mistakes Happen to Everybody

I waited patiently for the LORD,
He turned to me and heard my cry . . .
He made my feet steady.

❊ ❊ ❊

Psalm 40:1-2 ICB

When other people make mistakes, you must find a way to forgive them. And when you make mistakes, as you will from time to time, you must hope that other people will forgive you, too.

When you have done things that you regret, you should apologize, you should clean up the mess you've made, you should learn from your mistakes, and—last but not least—you should forgive yourself. Mistakes happen . . . it's simply a fact of life, and it's simply a part of growing up. So don't be too hard on yourself, especially if you've learned something along the way.

Made a mistake? Ask for forgiveness! If you've broken one of God's rules, you can always ask Him for His forgiveness. And He will always give it!

WOW

God is able to take mistakes and make something good out of them—something for our good and for His glory.

Ruth Bell Graham

When you fall short, ask for forgiveness: Nobody's perfect; no, not even you. When you make mistakes, as you most certainly will from time to time, ask for forgiveness, especially if you're seeking it from your kids. Your behavior will serve as a priceless example to your children.

Dear Lord,
sometimes I make mistakes.
When I do, forgive me, Father.
And help me learn from
my mistakes so that I can be
a better servant to You
and a better example
to my friends and family.

Amen

22

Practice, Practice, Practice

We say they are happy because
they did not give up. You have heard about
Job's patience, and you know the Lord's
purpose for him in the end. You know
the Lord is full of mercy and is kind.

❈ ❈ ❈

James 5:11 NCV

Forgiving other people requires practice and lots of it. So when it comes to forgiveness, here's something you should remember: if at first you don't succeed, don't give up!

Are you having trouble forgiving someone (or, for that matter, forgiving yourself for a mistake that you've made)? If so, remember that forgiveness isn't easy, so keep trying until you get it right . . . and if you keep trying, you can be sure that sooner or later, you will get it right.

You'll feel better! Forgiving other people is a good way to make yourself feel better. Why? First, when you forgive others, you know that you're obeying God, and that's a good feeling. Second, forgiveness is a great way to stop feeling angry—and that's a good feeling, too!

WOW

Because he never gave up,
the snail reached the ark.

C. H. Spurgeon

Parental practice: To become practiced in the art of forgiveness, you need practice. For most of us—kids and grown-ups alike—forgiveness doesn't come naturally. Keep practicing until it does.

Dear Lord,
when I have trouble forgiving
someone, when I'm discouraged
or tired or angry, let me turn
to You for strength,
for patience, for wisdom,
and for love.

Amen

23

Get over It!

Brothers and sisters, I know that I have
not yet reached that goal, but there
is one thing I always do. Forgetting
the past and straining toward what
is ahead, I keep trying to reach the goal
and get the prize for which God called me
through Christ to the life above.

❈ ❈ ❈

Philippians 3:13-14 NCV

An important part of learning how to forgive is learning how to get over the things that happened yesterday. What happened yesterday is past. And, if what happened yesterday has made you unhappy, today is as good a day as any to start getting over your hurt feelings.

Are you still angry with someone? Has that person said he was sorry and tried to make things better? If so, talk to your parents about it! They'll help you understand that you can't change the past, but you can get over it.

Tempted to fight? Walk away. The best fights are those that never happen.

WOW

Learning how to forgive and forget is one of the secrets of a happy Christian life.

Warren Wiersbe

Discuss the importance of forgiveness: Teach the importance of forgiveness every day and, if necessary, use words.

Dear Lord,
let me learn from what
happened yesterday, but don't
let me stay angry about what
happened yesterday. Let me
forgive others just as You have
forgiven me, and let me be
a happy, cheerful person
today and every day.

Amen

24

Do Yourself a Favor

I pray also that you will have greater
understanding in your heart . . .
and that you will know how rich
and glorious are the blessings God
has promised his holy people.

❀ ❀ ❀

Ephesians 1:18 NCV

When you forgive somebody else, you're actually doing yourself a favor. Why? Because when you forgive the other person, you get rid of angry feelings that can make you unhappy.

Are you still angry about something that happened yesterday, or the day before that, or the day before that? Do yourself a big favor: forgive everybody (including yourself, if necessary). When you do, you won't change what happened yesterday, but you will make today a whole lot better.

Do yourself another favor: Say it! If you love your brother or sister (and, of course, you do!) say so. But don't stop there: let all your family members know that you love them . . . a lot!

WOW
If we want to do something for God,
now is the time.
Vance Havner

Focused on the past? If so, it's time to refocus! If you want your child to appreciate the precious present—and you do—then live there.

Dear Lord,
make me a generous
and cheerful Christian.
Let me be kind to those who
need my encouragement,
and let me share with those
who need my help,
today and every day.

Amen

25

How Would Jesus Behave?

And be kind and compassionate to one another, forgiving one another, just as God also forgave you in Christ.

❋ ❋ ❋

Ephesians 4:32 HCSB

I t's easy to love people who have been nice to you, but it's very hard to love people who have treated you badly. Still, Jesus instructs us to treat both our friends and our enemies with kindness and respect.

Are you having problems being nice to someone? Is there someone you know whom you just don't like very much? Remember that Jesus not only forgave His enemies, He also loved them . . . and so should you.

If you're not sure that it's the right thing to do, don't do it! And if you're not sure that Jesus would approve of what you're about to say, don't say it.

WOW

Every Christian is to become
a little Christ. The whole purpose
of becoming a Christian
is simply nothing else.

C. S. Lewis

Parent Tip

It's up to us: Our children will learn about Jesus at church and, in some cases, at school. But, the ultimate responsibility for religious teachings should never be delegated to institutions outside the home. As parents, we must teach our children about the love and grace of Jesus Christ by our words and by our actions.

Dear Lord,
I am a very lucky person, and
I thank You for my blessings.
Help me to be a good person,
and help me use my talents and
my possessions for Your glory . . .
and for Your Son.

Amen

26 Forgiving Yourself!

The Lᴏʀᴅ says, "Forget what happened before. Do not think about the past. Look at the new thing I am going to do."

❋ ❋ ❋

Isaiah 43:18-19 ɪᴄʙ

*A*re you perfect? Of course not! Even if you're a very good person, you're bound to make mistakes and lots of them. And when you make a mistake, you should ask for forgiveness from a very important person: yourself!

After you've made a mistake, you'll probably feel sad, mad, bad—or a mixture of all three. When it happens, here are some things you can do:

1. Apologize to the people you've hurt;

2. Fix the things you've messed up or broken;

3. Don't make the same mistake again;

4. Ask God for His forgiveness (which, by the way, He will give to you instantly);

5. Forgive yourself;

6. Get busy doing something you can be proud of.

KiD TiP

You can make it right . . . if you think you can! If you've made a mistake, apologize. If you've broken something, fix it. If you've hurt someone's feelings, apologize. If you failed at something, try again. There is always something you can do to make things better . . . so do it!

WOW
If God had a refrigerator,
your picture would be on it.
Max Lucado

Parent Tip

When you make a mistake, admit it: No parent is perfect, not even you. Consequently, you will make mistakes from time to time (and yes, you might even lose your temper). When you make a mistake, apologize to the offended party, especially if that party is related to you by birth.

Dear Lord,
I have made mistakes,
and You have forgiven me.
Thank You for Your forgiveness.
When I am not perfect, help
other people to forgive me,
and help me forgive myself.

Amen

27 Pray about It!

Then if my people, who are called
by my name, are sorry for what they
have done, if they pray and obey me
and stop their evil ways, I will hear them
from heaven. I will forgive their sin,
and I will heal their land.

❈ ❈ ❈

2 Chronicles 7:14 NCV

If you are upset, pray about it. If there is a person you don't like, pray for a forgiving heart. If there is something you're worried about, ask God to comfort you. And as you pray more, you'll discover that God is always near and that He's always ready to hear from you. So don't worry about things; pray about them. God is always waiting . . . and listening!

Pray early and often: One way to make sure that your heart is in tune with God is to pray often. The more you talk to God, the more He will talk to you.

WOW
Prayer is never the least we can do;
it is always the most!
A. W. Tozer

Parents, too, must pray early and often: God is listening, and your children are watching.

Dear Lord,
whether I am feeling good
or bad, whether I am happy
or sad, I will pray. You always
hear my prayers, God;
let me always pray them!

Amen

28

Because It's the Right Thing to Do

Those who are pure in their thinking are happy, because they will be with God.

❋ ❋ ❋

Matthew 5:8 NCV

God gave you something called a conscience: it's that little feeling that tells you whether something is right or wrong. Your conscience will usually tell you what to do and when to do it. Trust that feeling.

If you stop to listen to your conscience, it won't be as hard for you to forgive people. Why? Because forgiving other people is the right thing to do. It's what God wants you to do. And it's what your conscience tells you to do. So what are you waiting for?

KID TIP

That little voice inside your head . . . is called your conscience. Listen to it; it's usually right!

WOW

God gives us a conscience and a Book—
the Bible. Let's make our decisions
day by day as we sense the leading of
His Spirit. This is how we grow.

Warren Wiersbe

Parent Tip

Sometimes, the little voice that we hear in our heads can be the echoes of our own parents' voices . . . and now that we're parents ourselves, we're the ones whose words will echo down through the hearts and minds of future generations. It's a big responsibility, but with God's help, we're up to the challenge.

Dear God,
You've given me a conscience
that tells me right from wrong.
Let me trust my conscience,
and let me live according
to Your teachings,
not just for today
but forever.

Amen

The Best Time to Forgive

So when you offer your gift to God
at the altar, and you remember that
your brother or sister has something
against you, leave your gift there at
the altar. Go and make peace with
that person, and then come
and offer your gift.

❋ ❋ ❋

Matthew 5:23-24 NCV

When is the best time to forgive somebody? Well, as the old saying goes, there's no time like the present. So if you have somebody you need to forgive, why not forgive that person today?

Forgiving other people is one of the ways that we make ourselves feel better. So if you're still angry about something that somebody did, forgive that person right now. There is no better time.

The time to forgive is now! God wants you to forgive people now, not later. Why? Because God knows that it's the right thing to do. And, of course, God wants you to be happy, not angry. God knows what's best for you, so if you have somebody you need to forgive, do it now.

WOW
If you're going to forgive somebody, why wait?

Marie T. Freeman

Bearing a grudge = bearing a burden: You know what a heavy burden it can be to bear a grudge against another person; make sure that your child knows, too!

Dear Lord,
whenever I am angry,
give me a forgiving heart.
And help me remember that
the best day to forgive
somebody is this one.

Amen

30

Because God Forgives Us

My whole being, praise the LORD
and do not forget all his kindnesses.
He forgives all my sins.

❈ ❈ ❈

Psalm 103:2-3 NCV

How often does God forgive us? More times than we can count! And that, by the way, is exactly how many times that God expects us to forgive other people—more times than we care to count.

Of this you can be sure: God won't ever get tired of forgiving you. And, because He has forgiven you, He doesn't want you to get tired of forgiving other people . . . ever!

God's love is forever! One of the most important lessons that you can ever learn is to trust God for everything. He loves you forever, and He will never let you down!

WOW
God loves each of us as if
there were only one of us.
St. Augustine

Reminder to moms and dads: There are many ways to say, "I love you." Find them. Put love notes in lunch pails and on pillows; hug relentlessly; laugh and play with abandon.

Dear Lord,
the Bible teaches me that
Your love lasts forever.
Thank You, God, for Your love.
Let me trust Your promises,
and let me live according to
Your teachings,
not just for today, but forever.

Amen

31

For God So Loved the World

For God loved the world in this way:
He gave His only Son, so that everyone
who believes in Him will not perish
but have eternal life.

❖ ❖ ❖

John 3:16 HCSB

How much does God love you? He loves you so much that He sent His Son Jesus to come to this earth for you! And, when you accept Jesus into your heart, God gives you a gift that is more precious than gold: that gift is called "eternal life," which means that you will live forever with God in heaven!

God's love is bigger and more powerful than anybody can imagine, but it is very real. So do yourself a favor right now: accept God's love with open arms and welcome His Son Jesus into your heart. When you do, your life will be changed today, tomorrow, and forever.

What a friend you have in Jesus: Jesus loves you, and He offers you eternal life with Him in heaven. Welcome Him into your heart. Now!

WOW

Tell me the story of Jesus.
Write on my heart every word.
Tell me the story most precious,
sweetest that ever was heard.

Fanny Crosby

Parent Tip

The Truth with a capital "T": Hannah Whitall Smith wrote, "The crucial question for each of us is this: What do you think of Jesus, and do you yet have a personal acquaintance with Him?" As parents, we must also ask ourselves another question: do our children know what we think about Jesus? And if not, why not?

Dear Lord,
thank You for loving me.
And thank You for sending
Your Son Jesus to this earth
so that I can receive the gifts
of eternal love and eternal life.
I will praise You, Dear God,
today, tomorrow, and forever.

Amen

Bible Verses to Memorize

Make a joyful shout to
the LORD, all you lands!
Serve the LORD
with gladness; Come
before His presence
with singing.

❋ ❋ ❋

Psalm 100:1-2 NKJV

The LORD is my shepherd;
I shall not want. He makes
me to lie down in green
pastures; He leads me
beside the still waters.
He restores my soul.

✳ ✳ ✳

Psalm 23:1-3 NKJV

I have come that they may have life, and that they may have it more abundantly.

■ ■ ■

John 10:10 NKJV

And Jesus said to them,
"I am the bread of life.
He who comes to Me
shall never hunger, and
he who believes in Me
shall never thirst."

❋ ❋ ❋

John 6:35 NKJV

Whoever does not love
does not know God,
because God is love.

❋ ❋ ❋

1 John 4:8 ICB

Do to others what you want them to do to you.

❊ ❊ ❊

Matthew 7:12 NCV

Now these three remain:
faith, hope, and love.
But the greatest
of these is love.

❊ ❊ ❊

1 Corinthians 13:13 HCSB

Draw near to God, and He will draw near to you.

❖ ❖ ❖

James 4:8 HCSB

We love Him because
He first loved us.

1 John 4:19 NKJV

Forgiveness

This is the day the LORD has made; we will rejoice and be glad in it.

❋ ❋ ❋

Psalm 118:24 NKJV

Jesus said to him,
"You shall love the LORD
your God with all your
heart, with all your soul,
and with all your mind.
This is the first and great
commandment.
And the second is like it:
'You shall love your
neighbor as yourself.'"

❈ ❈ ❈

Matthew 22:37-39 NKJV

I am able to do all things through Him who strengthens me.

❊ ❊ ❊

Philippians 4:13 HCSB

Let not your heart
be troubled;
you believe in God,
believe also in Me.

❊ ❊ ❊

John 14:1 NKJV

Be still, and know that I am God . . . .

❈ ❈ ❈

Psalm 46:10 KJV

For God so loved the world,
that he gave his only
begotten Son, that
whosoever believeth in
him should not perish,
but have everlasting life.

❋ ❋ ❋

John 3:16 KJV

For the LORD is good;
His mercy is everlasting,
and His truth endures
to all generations.

❋ ❋ ❋

Psalm 100:5 NKJV

Little Book Devotions help parents and children discuss important Biblical themes by relating those themes to the challenges of everyday life. These books are intended to be read *by* parents *to* children. Current titles include:

Little Book Devotions Honesty
Little Book Devotions Kindness
Little Book Devotions Patience
Little Book Devotions Forgiveness
Little Book Devotions Self-Control
Little Book Devotions Sharing

Additional titles are coming soon.

Little Book Devotions are available in LifeWay Christian Stores.